LEARNING
ABOUT LIBERTY

LEARNING ABOUT LIBERTY

The Cato University Study Guide

TOM G. PALMER

CATO
INSTITUTE
Washington, D.C.

ISBN 1-882577-66-3

Printed in the United States of America.

CATO INSTITUTE
1000 Massachusetts Ave., N.W.
Washington, D.C. 20001

Contents

General Introduction

Congratulations on enrolling in Cato University! You have embarked on a carefully paced program of study that we hope will provide you with greater knowledge and insight, as well as a deeper appreciation of the American heritage of constitutionally limited government and of the moral imperative of defending and advancing it.

This program has been designed to offer a comprehensive overview of the long and noble tradition of "classical liberal," or libertarian, thinking that informed the American Revolution and that informs the work of the Cato Institute today. It is offered only to Sponsors of the Cato Institute—people who, by becoming Sponsors, have demonstrated their commitment to the traditional American principles of limited government, individual liberty, and peace. Precisely because Cato's Sponsors are in the wealth-producing sector of society, they tend to be busy people, with many demands on their time. Accordingly, the curriculum of Cato University has been designed to allow such busy people the opportunity to delve deeply into the historical, philosophical, economic, legal, and moral foundations of the movement for individual liberty and limited government. The curriculum is built around two audiocassettes per module and a set of readings keyed to the issues raised in the audiocassettes. (The cassettes are sent monthly, allowing you to pace yourself at one module per month; if, however, you find that you "miss" a month, you have not "fallen behind," as this program is entirely self-paced.) This *Study Guide* indicates the "assigned" readings, all of which are drawn from books provided as part of your Cato University curriculum, as well as additional recommendations for those who wish to pursue particular subjects further.

You have received with this *Study Guide* two cassette tapes, a cassette binder capable of holding twenty-four tapes, and the following books:

Libertarianism: A Primer, by David Boaz

The Libertarian Reader, David Boaz, ed.
Freedom and the Law, by Bruno Leoni
Economics in One Lesson, by Henry Hazlitt
How the West Grew Rich, by Nathan Rosenberg and L. E. Birdzell Jr.
From Magna Carta to the Constitution: Documents in the Struggle for Liberty, David Brooks, ed.

The curriculum is divided into twelve modules; you will receive two cassettes every month. Of course, you can proceed at whatever pace you choose. We recommend that you follow the program in the sequence provided. Except for the first module, which provides a general thematic treatment of issues and thinkers that will be explored in greater detail in subsequent modules, the material is roughly chronological in order.

The twelve modules are as follows:

1. The Ideas of Liberty
2. John Locke's *Two Treatises of Government*
3. Thomas Paine's *Common Sense* and Thomas Jefferson and the Declaration of Independence
4. Adam Smith's *The Wealth of Nations* (Part I)
5. Adam Smith's *The Wealth of Nations* (Part II)
6. The Constitution of the United States of America
7. The Bill of Rights and Subsequent Amendments to the Constitution
8. John Stuart Mill's *On Liberty* and Mary Wollstonecraft's *Vindication of the Rights of Woman*
9. Henry David Thoreau's *Civil Disobedience* and William Lloyd Garrison's *The Liberator*
10. The Achievements of Nineteenth-Century Classical Liberalism
11. The "Austrian" Case for the Free Market
12. The Modern Quest for Liberty

The readings for each module are divided into three categories. The first category, "Readings to Accompany These Tapes," is items that are part of the library that you have received with this *Study Guide*. The second category, "Suggested Additional Reading," is mainly items that are not included in the library you received and is intended for those who want to learn more about the topics covered in the tapes and the first set of readings. The third category, "For Further Study," is intended for those with a very strong interest in learning more about the topics covered in the tapes and the associated readings. All of the items in the second and third categories are books, which should be available from most libraries; some are out of print and may be difficult to purchase. (For those that are in print, excellent sources are Laissez Faire Books, which can be reached at 938 Howard Street, Suite 202, San Francisco, California 94103, phone 800-326-0996, http://www.lfb.org, and Amazon.com, which can be reached at http://www.amazon.com.) No academic journal articles have been included, because they are normally difficult to obtain without access to a university research library.

We recommend that you first listen to the tapes and then undertake the readings, but that is by no means necessary. Each set of readings is followed by a short list of "Problems to Ponder" that deserve further thought.

Those who desire a more detailed guide to additional study are advised to consult the essay on "The Literature of Liberty" by Tom G. Palmer in *The Libertarian Reader*. For even more detail, or for suggestions on particular topics, please write to Tom G. Palmer at the Cato Institute, 1000 Massachusetts Avenue, N.W., Washington, D.C. 20001 (catouniversity@cato.org) and identify yourself as a Cato Institute Sponsor and Cato University enrollee.

Note: Some of the material presented in the tapes was commissioned specifically for Cato University; these include the tapes for modules 1, 10, and 12. Others were adapted from material that had been prepared by Knowledge Products, a division of Carmichael and Carmichael, a Sponsor of the Cato Institute; the scripts were written and edited by scholars associated with the Cato Institute. (Additional sophisticated audiotapes on the U.S. Constitution, philosophy, religion, political thought, morality, science and discovery, foreign affairs, and other topics are available from Knowledge Products, P. O. Box 100340, Nashville, Tennessee 37210, 1-800-876-4332 and e-mail kpaudio@edge.net. Be sure to mention that you are a Cato Institute Sponsor.)

Module 1: The Ideas of Liberty

The classical liberal, or libertarian, approach to morality and politics brings together related themes that will be both placed in their historical context and woven together more tightly in the coming modules. In this module, the basic ideas of individual and imprescriptible rights, spontaneous order, and the rule of law are presented and examined. Each of these ideas is implicated in the others: the spontaneous order of the free society is built on a foundation of secure individual rights, and law is intimately connected with liberty, for to be free in society is for all to be equally subjected to the same known law, a law that allows us to coordinate our activities with others and thus to create complex forms of social order. The deep roots of these ideas, reaching back into antiquity, give libertarianism a solidity other political philosophies lack.

Libertarianism draws on a multitude of different sciences, or organized bodies of knowledge, including history, philosophy, economics, sociology, anthropology, and law. Thus, "The Ideas of Liberty" devotes some attention to the status of the human sciences and to the meaning and importance of the principles of intentionality and methodological individualism in properly grounded social science. In addition to laying bare the scientific misunderstandings and equivocations that lie at the foundation of collectivist thinking, "The Ideas of Liberty" explores the relationships of the individual to the group, of action and design to order, of society to the state, of coercion to persuasion, and of "natural law" to "positive law." The ideas of natural law, natural rights, and "self-proprietorship" are traced through history, from the ancient Greeks to modern times, and used to illuminate the proper relationships between persons and between persons and governments. There is also a careful discussion of the relationship between "rights" thinking and "utilitarianism," which have been alleged by some philosophers to be mortal enemies. The confusion is eliminated by seeing "utility," or good consequences, as the goal, and rights as the standard against which policies and practice are judged.

Above all, libertarian ideas are seen as emerging from a long history, rather than as springing full-blown from the head of this or that particular philosopher. The treatment of the relationship between the "liberty of the ancients" and "the liberty of the moderns" by Benjamin Constant, included in the readings, is a clear statement of classical liberal thinking and a rebuttal to "communitarian" criticisms of liberal individualism.

Readings to Accompany These Tapes

From *Libertarianism: A Primer*: Chapter 1, "The Coming Libertarian Age" (pp. 1–26); Chapter 2, "The Roots of Libertarianism" (pp. 27–58).

From *The Libertarian Reader*: Introduction (pp. xi–xviii); Benjamin Constant, "The Liberty of the Ancients Compared with That of the Moderns" (pp. 65–70).

Suggested Additional Reading

From *How the West Grew Rich*: Introduction (pp. 3–36).

Charles Murray, *What It Means to Be a Libertarian: A Personal Interpretation* (New York: Broadway Books, 1997). This elegant short book sets out the arguments that persuaded a distinguished social scientist to adopt the libertarian perspective.

Milton Friedman, *Capitalism and Freedom* (Chicago: University of Chicago Press, 1962). This book changed the thinking of countless people who, through its pages, came to understand the intimate relationship between the free market and personal liberty.

For Further Study

Norman Barry, *On Classical Liberalism and Libertarianism* (New York: St. Martin's, 1987). This accessible little book presents an overview of classical liberal thinking, focusing almost entirely on twentieth-century thinkers.

F. A. Hayek, *The Constitution of Liberty* (Chicago: University of Chicago Press, 1960). This sometimes rather challenging book synthesizes Hayek's thinking on the relationships among individual rights, limited government, the rule of law, and the spontaneous order of a free society. The most interesting—and least dated—chapters are in Parts I and II (pp. 1–252) and the challenging postscript, "Why I Am Not a Conservative," in which Hayek argues for the principles of liberty as a guide to reform of the political order.

Western Liberalism: A History in Documents from Locke to Croce, E. K. Bramsted and K. J. Melhuish, eds. (New York: Longman, 1978). This brilliant collection includes both classical liberal writings and essays by some "revisionist" or "modern" liberal writers, such as T. H. Green and John Maynard Keynes.

Some Problems to Ponder

- What is the difference between "a Liberty for every Man to do what he lists" (Robert Filmer) and "a Liberty to dispose, and order, as he lists, his Person, Actions, Possessions, and his whole Property, within the Allowance of those Laws under which he is; and therein not to be subject to the arbitrary Will of another, but freely follow his own" (John Locke)? Is liberty the condition of being under no law whatsoever or the condition of being subject only to law that is equally applicable to all, rather than to the arbitrary will of others?
- What role does historical knowledge play in the grounding of libertarian ideas? How does "the lamp of experience" illuminate complex social, political, economic, and legal orders?
- How can a social science based on the intentionality of human action understand establishments that are the "result of human action, but not the execution of any human design" (Adam Ferguson)?
- How can "a human community that successfully claims the monopoly of the legitimate use of physical force within a given territory" (Max Weber) be brought under the rule of law? How useful—and how firm—is the distinction between "society" and the "state"?
- Are the "laws of economics," for example, that price controls tend to cause shortages and queues, part of the "natural law"?
- Could one defend individual liberty without appealing to the idea of "a property in one's person"?
- How are the statements "I *have a right* to do X" (an assertion of "subjective right") and "*It is right* that I be allowed to do X" (an assertion of "objective right") connected?

- What does it mean for a right to be "absolute" and "unconditional"? Does this mean that there are no conceivable circumstances under which it would not apply? Or are rights "contextual" and dependent upon certain conditions?

Module 2: John Locke's *Two Treatises of Government*

John Locke (1623–1704) was undoubtedly one of the most influential individuals who ever lived. Locke considered the great questions of slavery, religious toleration, constitutional government, individual rights, property, the market economy, and the foundations of justice. He was a physician, a philosopher, an economist, and an activist for liberty and limited government. He is also important as an "intellectual bridge" between the broader European civilization and the American revolutionaries whom his work inspired.

This module explores the foundation of Locke's thinking: the idea of the natural law, "an eternal law to all men," and his understanding of reason and our common "intellectual nature" as the foundation for the individual's "dominium" over himself or herself. Since "we are born free as we are born rational," restrictions or impositions upon our freedom require justification. "Being all equal and independent, no one ought to harm another in his life, health, liberty, or possessions." Each of us, Locke argued, has "a property in" his or her person, and that property is inalienable, that is, it cannot be transferred to another. Locke insisted that government cannot rest, as previous thinkers had argued, on the total transfer of the rights of the people to the sovereign, for the simple reason that some rights are by nature inalienable. Just as one cannot transfer one's moral responsibility for one's acts, one cannot alienate one's right over one's own life.

The true foundation of government rests in the consent of the people to the transfer of certain just powers to government in order to protect their rights, rather than in a total alienation of their rights to government. Government is made necessary by three deficiencies of the "state of nature": the lack of a known and settled law, the lack of a known and impartial judge to settle disputes, and the lack of a power to back and support the decisions of law. To remedy

9

these "inconveniences" of the state of nature, individuals delegate to government their right to execute the law of nature.

This module sets Locke's thinking in the context of the political conflicts of his time—notably over an established church and religious toleration, the powers and limitations of the sovereign, and the limits of governmental authority generally—and in the context of the philosophical currents and disputes of his time. The ideas of Hugo Grotius, Samuel Pufendorf, the Levellers (notably Richard Overton, whose essay is excerpted in the readings for this module), Algernon Sidney, Robert Filmer (the apologist for absolutist government whom Locke and Sidney set out to refute), and others are examined and compared with Locke's ideas.

Locke's writings helped to set the stage for the modern world, including legal protections for individual rights and constitutionally limited representative government. Most modern thinking bears the trace of Locke's influence. Locke's approach has been updated and applied to the problem of "justice in holdings" by Robert Nozick and applied to more concrete problems by David Boaz in his chapter "What Rights Do We Have?"

Readings to Accompany These Tapes

From *The Libertarian Reader*: John Locke, "Understanding Can Not Be Compelled" (pp. 53–57) and "Of Property and Government" (pp. 123–39); Richard Overton, "An Arrow against All Tyrants" (pp. 121–22); Robert Nozick, "The Entitlement Theory of Justice" (pp. 181–96).

From *Libertarianism: A Primer*: Chapter 3, "What Rights Do We Have?" (pp. 59–93).

From *From Magna Carta to the Constitution: Documents in the Struggle for Liberty*: "Agreement of the Free People of England" (1649) (pp. 25–36).

Suggested Additional Reading

John Locke, *Two Treatises of Government*. Although a variety of editions of this classic work are available, the most highly recommended is the one edited by Peter Laslett, which provides useful notes and an introduction. The Second Treatise is well worth reading in its entirety, both to appreciate the logic of its arguments and to experience for oneself the rigor of Locke's libertarian, or Whig, arguments for liberty.

Stephen Buckle, *Natural Law and the Theory of Property: Grotius to Hume* (Oxford: Oxford University Press, 1991). This very readable and appealing book traces the ideas of natural law and of private property, with an especially interesting chapter on Locke.

A. John Simmons, *The Lockean Theory of Rights* (Princeton: Princeton University Press, 1992) and *On the Edge of Anarchy: Locke, Consent, and the Limits of Society* (Princeton: Princeton University Press, 1993). These two books attempt to restate Locke's arguments in modern philosophical terms, to explicate their meaning, and to apply them to contemporary problems in moral and political philosophy. The reasoning and writing are clear, even if it sometimes seems that Simmons takes special pains to distinguish Locke from the libertarian tradition of which he is so clearly a part.

For Further Study

Algernon Sidney, *Discourses Concerning Government*, Thomas G. West, ed. (1698; Indianapolis: Liberty Classics, 1990). Like Locke's *Two Treatises of Government*, Sidney's work was written as a response to the arguments for unlimited royal government and served as a powerful inspiration to the American Founders, who referred to Sidney as "Sidney the Martyr," because he was executed for plotting to kill Charles II. Sidney's papers, including a draft of the *Discourses*, were used as evidence against him. Although there is nothing in the work that is incompatible with constitutional monarchy, the indictment of Sidney claimed that the *Discourses* were a "false, seditious, and traitorous libel," citing sentences that stated that the king is subject to law and accountable to the people.

Richard Ashcraft, *Revolutionary Politics and Locke's Two Treatises of Government* (Princeton: Princeton University Press, 1986). This book provides a thorough introduction to the political background of Locke's writings and reveals the radicalism of Locke's views on the legitimacy of government, as well as recounting his intense political activism on behalf of the Whig cause.

Joyce Oldham Appleby, *Economic Thought and Ideology in Seventeenth-Century England* (Princeton: Princeton University Press, 1978). This book explains the background from which emerged the philosophy of limited government, free markets, and a self-ordering society.

Some Problems to Ponder

- What is the difference between the "state of nature" and life in political society? If I am in a political society with one person, can I still be in a state of nature with regard to another? What is the difference between Locke's state-of-nature theory and Hobbes's state-of-nature theory, with which it is sometimes confused?

- What does it mean to say that the "state of nature" has a "law of nature" to govern it?

- What would be objectionable, from a Lockean libertarian perspective, about "selling oneself into slavery"? In addition to Locke's theological arguments (that we are God's property and therefore cannot sell ourselves), is there a secular argument to the same effect?

- What does Richard Overton mean when he writes, "To every individual in nature is given an individual property by nature, not to be invaded or usurped by any; for everyone as he is himself, so he hath a self-propriety, else could he not be himself"? How could one "not be himself"?

- Is there a difference between the thievery of a petty thief and the taxation policies of government? What about the "taxation policies" of a condominium association that assesses monthly "condo fees" for maintenance of the building, garden, and so forth?

- How does "mixing one's labour" with naturally occurring resources generate an exclusive property in them?

- What is the difference between "negative community" (an equal right to appropriate) and "positive community" (an equal right to common management or to a share of the common product)? Is the distinction relevant to Locke's argument about the emergence and justification of private property rights?

- What is the difference between "express consent" and "tacit consent"? If unanimous consent is the best guarantor of the rights of all, but difficult to obtain, how does majority consent serve as a "second-best" alternative? Are there limits to what the majority may consent to?

- What does it mean to say that, in cases of just rebellion, it is not the people who have rebelled against their rulers but the rulers who have rebelled against the people?
- What is liberty? Is it the absence of all constraint whatsoever, as some believe, or freedom from the arbitrary will of other humans?
- Once the people have consented to a government, have they consented to submit to whatever that government does?

Module 3: Thomas Paine's *Common Sense* and Thomas Jefferson and the Declaration of Independence

The American Revolution is all too often confused with the War for Independence. As John Adams noted in a letter of 1815 to Thomas Jefferson, "What do we mean by the Revolution? The war? That was no part of the Revolution; it was only an effect and consequence of it. The Revolution was in the minds of the people, and this was effected, from 1760 to 1775, in the course of fifteen years before a drop of blood was drawn at Lexington. The records of thirteen legislatures, the pamphlets, newspapers in all the colonies, ought to be consulted during that period to ascertain the steps by which the public opinion was enlightened and informed concerning the authority of Parliament over the colonies." This lesson examines the "Revolution in the minds of the people" that Adams described, focusing on Thomas Paine's remarkably influential pamphlet *Common Sense*, published in January 1776 and reprinted twenty-five times in the next year, and the Declaration of Independence that it helped to inspire.

Thomas Paine (1737–1809) wrote several books and pamphlets that greatly contributed to "delegitimizing" the claims to authority of the British state. Paine asserted that "society in every state is a blessing, but government, even in its best state, is but a necessary evil; in its worst state an intolerable one" and directed the reader to the discussion of the nature of rulers in the Bible (I Samuel 8, included in the readings for this module). As to the particular claims of the British monarchy, Paine noted, "No man in his senses can say that their claim under William the Conqueror is a very honorable one. A French bastard, landing with an armed banditti and establishing himself king of England against the consent of the natives, is in plain terms a very paltry rascally original. It certainly hath no divinity in it."

The Declaration of Independence is more than a mere declaration of intention to sever political ties with Britain. It is a carefully crafted argument justifying that intention. It ranks as one of the greatest and most influential political documents of all time. (One of thirty-two surviving copies made in 1823 directly from the original Declaration, using ink lifted from the surface of the parchment, hangs in the lobby of the Cato Institute building in Washington, D.C.) When the Founders offered a careful set of arguments for armed revolution, they were fully aware of the consequences. That course was not undertaken lightly. When he signed a document that concluded, "We mutually pledge to each other our Lives, our Fortunes, and our sacred Honor," each signatory knew that he was signing his own death warrant in the event of failure.

The material in this module reveals the way in which the American experiment in liberty and limited government arose out of the intersection of libertarian moral and political philosophy and the political conflicts of the day, for example, the intersection of support for freedom of trade and attempts by the British government to impose mercantilist policies on the Americans in the interest of the British East Indies Company. A particularly important topic discussed in this module is the glaring contradiction between the claims to liberty and self-government made by the revolutionaries and the existence of the degrading practice of chattel slavery in many of the colonies.

Thomas Jefferson (1743–1826), in drafting the Declaration of Independence, had, as he later said, "turned to neither book nor pamphlet in writing it"; he attempted simply "to place before mankind the common sense of the subject." This is strong evidence of the degree to which libertarian ideas, such as those articulated by John Locke in the previous century, had come to permeate popular American thinking on morality and politics. It is notable how many of the phrases from Locke's *Second Treatise of Government* are echoed in the Declaration of Independence.

In addition to the Declaration of Independence and excerpts from Paine's writings, the readings for this module include the Declarations of the Stamp Act Congress and of the First Continental Congress, setting out the grievances of the American colonists.

The most enduring legacy of the American Revolution is the attempt to establish a system of individual liberty and limited government under law—a system consistent with the nature of human beings as moral agents with inalienable rights. That effort has been an inspiration to lovers of liberty all around the globe.

Readings to Accompany These Tapes

From *The Libertarian Reader*: The Bible, I Samuel 8 (pp. 5–6); Thomas Paine, "Of the Origin and Design of Government" (pp. 7–12) and "Of Society and Civilization" (pp. 211–14).

From *From Magna Carta to the Constitution: Documents in the Struggle for Liberty*: Declarations of the Stamp Act Congress (1765) (pp. 47–50), Declaration of the First Continental Congress (1774) (pp. 51–56), Declaration of Independence (1776) (pp. 51–62).

Suggested Additional Reading

Thomas Paine, *Political Writings*, Bruce Kuklick, ed. (Cambridge: Cambridge University Press, 1989). This book brings together Paine's most influential works: *Common Sense; The Crisis, Number 1; The Rights of Man, Part I; The Rights of Man, Part II;* and *The Age of Reason, Part First*.

Thomas Jefferson, *The Portable Thomas Jefferson*, Merrill D. Peterson, ed. (New York: Viking Press, 1977). This edition includes in its version of the Declaration of Independence the sections deleted from Jefferson's draft, including his condemnation of the slave trade. Other important writings of Jefferson include "A Summary View of the Rights of British America," "The Kentucky Resolutions" (in which Jefferson asserted that "free government is founded in jealousy, and not in confidence; it is jealousy and not confidence which prescribes limited constitutions, to bind down those whom we are obliged to trust with power"), and the "First Inaugural Address" (in which Jefferson asked, after listing the advantages enjoyed by the inhabitants of America, "With all these blessings, what more is necessary to make us a happy and prosperous people? Still one thing more, fellow citizens—a wise and frugal government, which shall restrain men from injuring one another, which shall leave them otherwise free to regulate their own pursuits of industry and improvement, and shall not take from the mouth of labor the bread it has earned. This is the sum of good government, and this is necessary to close the circle of our felicities").

Carl Becker, *The Declaration of Independence: A Study in the History of Political Ideas* (1922; New York: Random House, 1958). A distinguished historian neatly explains such matters as the philosophical antecedents to the Declaration, the principles of natural law, and the then-current theory of the British Empire and offers a careful examination of the rhetoric and language of the Declaration itself. This short but brilliant book is inspiring.

David N. Mayer, *The Constitutional Thought of Thomas Jefferson* (Charlottesville: University of Virginia Press, 1995). This book examines Jefferson's views on the fundamental constitutional questions about the relationship of the individual to government, the states to the federal government, and more. Rather than mischaracterizing Jefferson as an "agrarian," Mayer examines Jefferson's thought on Jefferson's own terms—as "Whig," "federal," and "republican." He tells how, steeped in English common law doctrines, Jefferson developed a distinctly American philosophy of law. He describes Jefferson's ideas for reforming criminal law, the immortal principles Jefferson expressed in the Declaration of Independence, his advocacy of a bill of rights, and his performance as president. This is an important addition to the literature on the early American republic.

For Further Study

Bernard Bailyn, *The Ideological Origins of the American Revolution* (Cambridge, Mass: Harvard University Press, 1967). A distinguished American historian examines in great detail the intellectual background of the American Revolution.

John Trenchard and Thomas Gordon, *Cato's Letters: Essays on Liberty*, edited and annotated by Ronald Hamowy (Indianapolis: Liberty Classics, 1995). These essays popularized Locke's ideas and were profoundly influential in both England and America. They are the inspiration for the Cato Institute. Published anonymously in the *London Journal* from 1720 to 1723, the 144 letters provide a compelling theoretical basis for freedom of conscience and freedom of speech. Virtually half the private libraries in the American colonies contained bound volumes of *Cato's Letters*.

The English Libertarian Heritage, David L. Jacobson, ed., with a new foreword by Ronald Hamowy (San Francisco: Fox & Wilkes, 1994).

This is an accessible collection of the various writings that influenced the American Founders, notably the most relevant of *Cato's Letters*.

Peter Ackerman and Christopher Kruegler, *Strategic Nonviolent Conflict: The Dynamics of People Power in the Twentieth Century* (New York: Praeger, 1993). The authors offer a thoughtful and careful consideration of resistance theory, with well-developed case studies. This book provides a useful update and application of the theories of resistance to tyranny that were commonly discussed in the eighteenth century.

Some Problems to Ponder

- To what extent were the American revolutionaries defending a tradition of liberty and constitutionalism against encroaching absolutism, and to what extent were they introducing and implementing new principles?
- Were the colonists of British America being "ungrateful" for the protection offered them by the British Empire during, for example, the French and Indian Wars? To what extent does the extension of protection of the sort offered by the British armies obligate the protected?
- What is the distinction between resistance to unjust authority and active revolution seeking to overturn unjust authority? What might justify revolution to "alter or abolish" an established authority?
- What is the role of representation in legitimizing political authority?
- What is the distinction between an alienable right and an *in*alienable right?
- In what way(s) might a legitimate government rest upon the "consent of the governed"?
- How has popular political thinking changed since the time of Paine and Jefferson? In what ways has it become more libertarian, and in what ways less?
- What distinctly Lockean elements can be identified in the Declaration of Independence?

Module 4: Adam Smith's *The Wealth of Nations* (Part I)

Adam Smith (1723–1790) was not the first to try to understand the market economy, but he may have been the most influential and eloquent observer of economic life. His observation that a person may be "led by an invisible hand to promote an end that was no part of his intention" became the guiding star of an investigation of the beneficial unintended consequences of voluntary exchange, an investigation that still continues strong after more than 200 years. (Others had reached that insight earlier, as the excerpt from the *Tao Te Ching* of Lao-tzu in the readings indicates; interestingly, the writings of Lao-tzu were distributed by the anti-Nazi White Rose group in Germany to undercut the National Socialist regime.)

In addition to seeking to explain how markets work and how order emerges spontaneously from the voluntary interactions of countless market participants, Smith was very concerned with understanding how virtue fares in commercial society. He saw how commercial relations tend to encourage probity, punctuality, and honesty in dealings. As he observed, "Of all the nations in Europe, the Dutch, the most commercial, are the most faithful to their word." He argued that this was not due to some unique Dutch national characteristic or racial distinction but was

> far more reduceable to self interest, that general principle which regulates the action of every man, and which leads men to act in a certain manner from views of advantage, and is as deeply planted in an Englishman as a Dutchman. A dealer is afraid of losing his character, and is scrupulous in observing every engagement. When a person makes perhaps twenty contracts in a day, he cannot gain so much by endeavouring to impose on his neighbors, as the very appearance of a cheat would make him lose. Where people seldom deal with one another, we find that they are somewhat disposed to cheat, because they can gain more by a smart trick than they can lose by the injury which it does their character.

21

Smith follows up this observation with a dry remark that certainly rings true: "They whom we call politicians are not the most remarkable men in the world for probity and punctuality."

Enemies of free-market relationships tend to portray voluntary exchanges as "zero sum," that is, a gain to one party can come only at a loss to the other. But Smith showed how trade is based on mutual benefit, rather than conflict over fixed resources. The division of labor, so bemoaned by socialists as the source of "alienation," is seen as the foundation for an enormous system of social cooperation and wealth production. Among Adam Smith's accomplishments in changing how people think about wealth was his redefinition of "nation"; not only privileged members of the court, but every human being counted as a part of a nation. Eliminating special privileges may be to the short-run detriment of special interests, but free markets and the attendant economic progress and growth are to the long-term benefit of all the members of society, including the least powerful, whose interests count as much as those of the powerful.

A common criticism of classical liberalism is that it focuses too much on the abstract rules of justice, which are, communitarian critics allege, the principles appropriate for abstract men. Benevolence, love, national identity, or some other principle, they believe, would be the proper foundation for a good human society. Smith responded to this criticism in *The Theory of Moral Sentiments* (excerpted in the readings), and David Boaz examines the issue in his chapter on "Civil Society" in *Libertarianism: A Primer*.

An Inquiry into the Nature and Causes of the Wealth of Nations, published in the same year as the American Declaration of Independence, is one of the great books of the classical liberal tradition, and one that continues to instruct us in the principles and functioning of the free society.

Readings to Accompany These Tapes

From *Libertarianism: A Primer*: Chapter 7, "Civil Society" (pp. 127–47); Chapter 8, "The Market Process" (pp. 148–85).

From *The Libertarian Reader*: Adam Smith, "Justice and Beneficence" (pp. 58–61), "The Man of System" (pp. 209–10), "The Division of Labor" (pp. 253–54), "Society and Self-Interest" (pp. 256–57); David Hume, "Justice and Property" (pp. 135–39); Lao-tzu, "Harmony" (pp. 207–8).

Suggested Additional Reading

Adam Smith, *An Inquiry into the Nature and Causes of the Wealth of Nations* (many editions) and *The Theory of Moral Sentiments* (many editions). The most elegant and scholarly—and certainly the most affordable—editions of the works of Adam Smith are the paperback editions from Liberty Press. These two works reveal Smith the economist and Smith the moral philosopher and show the relationships between the two ways of viewing humanity.

David Hume, *Essays: Moral, Political, and Literary* (various editions). Hume was a close friend and collaborator of Adam Smith, and he expressed complementary views in his various books and essays. Of special relevance to this module are the essays "Of the Balance of Trade" and "Of the Jealousy of Trade."

E. G. West, *Adam Smith: The Man and His Works* (Indianapolis: Liberty Fund, 1976). West offers a sympathetic and enlightening overview of Adam Smith's ideas.

For Further Study

Ronald Hamowy, *The Scottish Enlightenment and the Theory of Spontaneous Order* (Carbondale: Southern Illinois University Press, 1987). Hamowy presents a general introduction to the Scottish Enlightenment, the period in the late eighteenth century when such Scottish luminaries as Adam Ferguson, Adam Smith, Francis Hutcheson, and David Hume dazzled the world with the brilliance of their thought, and the central role played in it by the idea of spontaneous order.

T. S. Ashton, *The Industrial Revolution, 1760–1830* (Oxford: Oxford University Press, 1962). In a compact presentation, this distinguished economic historian documents the beneficial effects of the Industrial Revolution, which created widespread wealth on a scale never before imaginable, and refutes the many myths about how capitalism and industrialism made the masses miserable.

Neil McKendrick, John Brewer, and J. H. Plumb, *The Birth of a Consumer Society: The Commercialization of Eighteenth-Century England* (Bloomington: Indiana University Press, 1982). This brilliant work documents the rise of an economy oriented toward satisfying willing buyers, in which, as Neil McKendrick notes, "There were profits—even small fortunes—to be made from very modest artefacts indeed. It is no accident that Adam Smith's famous example of the division of labour was taken from the manufacture of pins."

Some Problems to Ponder

- If "nothing could be more absurd" than the doctrine of the "balance of trade," as Smith noted, why has this doctrine persisted and continued to dominate most public discussions of trade policy?
- Which is of primary importance or absolutely necessary for the maintenance of society, benevolence or justice?
- Many people who are hostile to the free market assert that commerce undercuts or erodes moral relations; they believe that people are encouraged by market exchange to think of each other solely as competitors or as sources of benefits, rather than as friends and neighbors, so that "profits" replace affection, goodness, and morality. Smith argues, to the contrary, that commerce encourages the virtues of honesty and fair dealing and that those are the foundations for the flourishing of the other virtues. How could we determine which view is right?
- Adam Smith wrote *An Inquiry into the Nature and Causes of the Wealth of Nations*. What, for Adam Smith, is a nation?
- A nightly news reporter announces, "The administration today made major concessions in international trade negotiations by agreeing to open American markets to imports of foreign goods." What might Adam Smith or other economists say about that way of understanding trade relations and policies?

Module 5: Adam Smith's *The Wealth of Nations* (Part II)

Adam Smith was both moral philosopher and social scientist. He sought to understand the wellsprings of morality as well as the regulating principles of social life. In seeking to understand the natural laws governing the regularities of economic life, Smith took the time to observe carefully how business enterprises operated, how markets were organized, and how the prices at which goods were exchanged were determined. Working out the relationships of "supply and demand" that determine prices in the market was one of his principal concerns. Despite his flawed theory of value, Smith did much to explain how the "higgling and haggling" of the market results in prices that coordinate complex economic and social undertakings. From barter, the important institution of money, in the form of precious metals that are "fit to be the instruments of commerce and circulation," emerges, greatly increasing the possibilities of mutually beneficial exchange and social coordination.

In this module, the results of Smith's investigations of the natural rules or laws of exchange are explained and then reinterpreted in light of the "marginal revolution" of the 1870s, which allowed Smith's enterprise to be put on much more secure footing. An important insight that has survived unchanged, however, is Smith's crucial distinction between "effectual demand" and "absolute demand." When someone says, "I want X," thereby expressing an "absolute demand," we learn less than if he were to explain how much he is actually willing to give up for a unit of X, that is, his "effectual demand." "More health and safety" are undoubtedly desirable, but the important question is, "How much convenience, pleasure, or other goods would you give up for another increment of health or safety?"

To overcome the natural poverty of mankind, Smith emphasized, there must be growth in the capital stock. Capital accumulation changes the ratio of labor to capital, meaning that an additional unit of labor can produce more wealth than before, thus raising the living standards of the working masses of the population. Those who are concerned about poverty must be concerned about increasing the stock of capital; increasing the stock of capital is the only way to increase living standards. As Adam Smith and subsequent generations of economists have shown, the free market is probably the most humanitarian institution the human race has ever produced.

What is necessary for wealth creation to proceed and for the attendant rise in living standards is not availability of more natural resources; many resource-poor places are inhabited by rich populations, while many resource-rich places are inhabited by poor populations. Good institutions, such as a secure system of private property, freedom of contract, and the rule of law, are necessary for wealth to be produced, as Rosenberg and Birdzell show in the reading from their book.

Readings to Accompany These Tapes

From *The Libertarian Reader*: Adam Smith, "Labor and Commerce" (pp. 258–59), "Free Trade" (pp. 260–62), "The Simple System of Natural Liberty" (pp. 263–64).

From *How the West Grew Rich*: Chapter 4, "The Evolution of Institutions Favorable to Commerce" (pp. 113–43).

Suggested Additional Reading

Joseph Schumpeter, *History of Economic Analysis* (Oxford: Oxford University Press, 1954). Schumpeter's work is a magisterial treatment of its topic; it places Adam Smith in the context of other writers and of what they and Smith set out to explain.

Thomas Sowell, *Classical Economics Reconsidered* (Princeton: Princeton University Press, 1994). With scholarly precision Sowell sympathetically reconstructs the principal ideas of the classical economists, including Adam Smith. One of the more interesting parts of his treatment is the attention he devotes to the classical economists' concern with promoting economic growth as the key to prosperity for the masses of the population.

For Further Study

Edwin G. West, *Adam Smith and Modern Economics: From Market Behaviour to Public Choice* (Cheltenham, U.K.: Edward Elgar, 1990).

West places Adam Smith's work in the context of modern economic science and demonstrates the continuing relevance of Smith's work, two centuries after his death, with special emphasis on the inspiration he has given to economic research during the last two decades.

Carl Menger, *Principles of Economics* (1871; New York: New York University Press, 1981). This book was one of the three books published in the 1870s that revolutionized economics by focusing on the "marginal" unit as the unit of choice that determines exchange relationships (prices). While agreeing with much of what Smith had argued, Menger put economics on a more secure foundation than had Smith.

Some Problems to Ponder

- Why do humans bargain and trade? What is unique, among all the creatures of whom we have any knowledge, about humans that makes exchange both possible and a necessity of life?
- How does a barter economy evolve into an economy in which exchanges are mediated by money? What is the role of money in facilitating exchange and voluntary coordination of activities? What makes commodities "fit to be the instruments of commerce and circulation"?
- How does capital accumulation, or growth in the capital stock, increase the productivity and wages of labor?
- How did the contributors to the "marginal revolution" in economics improve on Adam Smith's explanation of the workings of supply and demand? How does the focus on the marginal unit affect our understanding of public policy, for example, of how legally mandated increases in minimum wages can cause unemployment?
- Are markets characterized only by competition? What about cooperation? What is the relationship between competition and cooperation?

Module 6: The Constitution of the United States of America

The Constitution of the United States of America is part of a long line of charters written and implemented to establish strictly limited governmental power that is nonetheless strong enough to secure the rights of the people. As the fundamental law of the land, the text of the Constitution should be known by every American citizen.

In this module, the historical background to the proposal for a new Constitution is examined in detail, as well as the text of the Constitution itself and the struggle between its opponents and its advocates over ratification. The result was by no means a simple victory for advocates of a new national constitution; it was something quite different, a result shaped as much by Anti-Federalists as by Federalists. The Constitution as adopted incorporated the Bill of Rights capped by an explicit statement of the limited nature of the powers accorded to the federal government.

In seeking to establish a government powerful enough to secure the rights of the people, the Framers had to confront the problem of how to limit that power and constrain it from expanding whenever expansion might be in the interest of the most powerful factions. To secure that end, the Framers applied the doctrines of the separation of powers, or of "checks and balances," and maintained the independence of state governments. In addition, such mechanisms as the staggered six-year terms of the Senate were designed to temper policy and to insulate it from occasional paroxysms of popular sentiment.

The most profound political thinking and writing are usually called forth during great political and legal conflicts. The debates over the Articles of Confederation and the Constitution proposed as a substitute for them are no exception. *The Federalist Papers* and the various lesser known Anti-Federalist Papers exhibit an extraordinary degree of practical and philosophical sophistication.

This module examines both sides of what is perhaps the most important issue dividing Americans today, one that is still hotly debated in American jurisprudence: does the government have all the powers it might wish to claim, except those specifically denied it in the Constitution, or does it have only those powers specifically enumerated in the Constitution?

Readings to Accompany These Tapes

From *From Magna Carta to the Constitution: Documents in the Struggle for Liberty*: Articles of Confederation (1778) (pp. 63–74); Constitution of the United States of America (1789) (pp. 75–89).

From *The Libertarian Reader*: James Madison, "Federalist Number Ten" (pp. 13–19); Richard Epstein, "Self-Interest and the Constitution" (pp. 42–52).

From *Libertarianism: A Primer*: Chapter 6, "Law and the Constitution" (pp. 115–26).

Suggested Additional Reading

Roger Pilon, "Restoring Constitutional Government," *Cato's Letter* No. 9 (Washington: Cato Institute, 1995). This pamphlet, available from the Cato Institute, explains how the Constitution established a government of delegated, enumerated, and thus limited, powers and how to restore such constitutional government today.

Alexander Hamilton, James Madison, and John Jay, *The Federalist Papers* (many editions). Few people read *The Federalist Papers* in their entirety; many were written on topics of little interest today or on very specific issues of the Constitution then being debated. The papers that definitely deserve special attention today include No. 1 (introduction to the structure and objectives of the papers); No. 10 (union as a safeguard against domestic faction and insurrection—included in *The Libertarian Reader*); No. 45 (ensuring that the powers and rights of the states have been maintained); No. 46 (ensuring that the states have been left ample power to counteract an ambitious national government); No. 47 (arguing for the separation of powers); No. 48 (arguing that overlapping powers facilitate separation of powers); No. 51 (arguing for checks and balances, reinforcing the separation of powers through self-interest); No. 78 (arguing for the powers of the judiciary to protect us—via judicial review—from majoritarian excesses); and No. 84

(arguing that the doctrine of enumerated powers renders a bill of rights unnecessary).

The Anti-Federalists: Writings by the Opponents of the Constitution, Herbert J. Storing, ed. (Chicago: University of Chicago Press, 1985). As Herbert Storing and other scholars have pointed out, the so-called Anti-Federalists have an equal claim to being the authors of our constitutional system, through their insistence on the doctrine of enumerated powers and on the Bill of Rights, including the Ninth and Tenth Amendments. Some of the more relevant papers, warning of the dangers of centralized powers and stressing the need for decentralization and legal guarantees against the abuse of power, include the Letter from "Centinel" (pp. 13–20); Letters from "A Federal Farmer" (pp. 32–95); Essays of "Brutus," 18 October 1787 (pp. 108–17) (contrasting confederal with national government), 29 November 1787 (pp. 127–32) (on the powers of Congress), 13 December 1787 (pp. 133–38), 31 January 1788, 7 February 1788, 14 February 1788, 21 February 1788, 28 February 1788, 6 March 1788, and 20 March 1788 (pp. 162–87) (on judicial powers); 10 April 1788 (pp. 187–91) (on the Senate); Letters of "Agrippa," 23 November 1787 (pp. 229–30) (contrasting limited government with absolute government), 14 December 1787 (pp. 239–40) (on the need for a "declaration of rights").

For Further Study

Stephen Macedo, *The New Right vs. the Constitution* (Washington: Cato Institute, 1987). Macedo carefully examines the original intent jurisprudence of the "new right" school of constitutional interpretation, which argues for an essentially untrammeled majoritarianism. Macedo argues for interpreting the Constitution in light of the theory of rights and government that inspired the Founders, rather than as merely a structure for the exercise of democratic power.

Edwin S. Corwin, *The "Higher Law" Background of American Constitutional Law* (Ithaca: Cornell University Press, 1955). Corwin shows how the American Constitution rests on a foundation of natural and inalienable individual rights.

From *The Libertarian Reader*: Lysander Spooner, "The Constitution of No Authority" (pp. 154-60). This essay pushes to the limit the idea of a government based on the consent of the governed and

raises important and difficult problems concerning the foundations of political authority, with special attention to the U.S.
Constitution.

Some Problems to Ponder

- In Article I, Section 8, of the Constitution, the Congress is
  granted the power "To make all Laws which shall be necessary
  and proper for carrying into Execution the foregoing Powers,
  and all other Powers vested by this Constitution in the Government of the United States, or in any Department or Officer
  thereof." What role do the terms "necessary" and "proper"
  play in this clause?
- James Madison, in Federalist No. 10, addresses the problem of
  limiting the power of majority factions. His answer was not to
  eliminate the *causes* of faction, for that would mean eliminating
  liberty and even human nature itself, but to seek "relief . . . only
  . . . in the means of controlling its *effects*." A national government, Madison argued, would be more likely to secure republican liberty from the dangers of majority faction than would
  local government only: "Extend the sphere, and you take in a
  greater variety of parties and interests; you make it less probable
  that a majority of the whole will have a common motive to
  invade the rights of other citizens; or if such a common motive
  exists, it will be more difficult for all who feel it to discover
  their own strength, and to act in unison with each other." In
  protecting against the danger of *majority* faction, however, did
  Madison at the same time open the door to *minority* faction, or
  what we today term "special interests"? Did Madison's solution
  also make it more difficult to motivate a majority, for example,
  taxpayers, with a "common motive" to protect their rights
  against minorities, in this case, subsidized special interests?
  What constitutional innovations or amendments might guard
  against both majority *and* minority tyranny?
- Is there a distinction between judicial review and nullification
  of unconstitutional laws, on the one hand, and judicial lawmak-
  ing or usurpation of the legislative power, on the other? Are
  there other mechanisms, in addition to judicial review, to com-
  bat or resist usurpation of or encroachment on the rights of the
  people by the other branches of government?

• In Article I, Section 8, of the Constitution, the Congress is granted power to "lay and collect Taxes, Duties, Imposts and Excises, to pay the Debts and provide for the common Defence and general Welfare of the United States. . . ." Does this mean that the Congress has been granted the power to take any act it believes will "provide for the . . . general Welfare"? Is there a contrast between "general welfare" and "particular welfare"? Is the term "general" a limiting or an empowering term? What is the meaning of this section?

Module 7: The Bill of Rights and Subsequent Amendments to the Constitution

The fight over ratification of the Constitution was won by its proponents, the Federalists, only by means of a compromise with their opponents, the Anti-Federalists. That compromise was the addition of the Bill of Rights, the first ten amendments to the Constitution. The fear of a consolidated government was by no means new or unique to Americans; it grew out of a long history of struggles to limit the powers of kings, going back at least to Magna Carta. The various efforts to tie the rulers down with constitutional chains are charted in the audiocassettes for this module and documented in the readings, including Magna Carta, the Petition of Right, and the English Bill of Rights. Fear of expanding government is not out-of-date, as David Boaz demonstrates in his chapter "What Big Government Is All About."

The audiocassettes for this module explain the background and meaning of each of the amendments in the Bill of Rights, as well as the debates over their ratification. In addition, all of the subsequent amendments to the Constitution are examined and explained.

Readings to Accompany These Tapes

From *From Magna Carta to the Constitution: Documents in the Struggle for Liberty*: Magna Carta (1215) (pp. 1–16); the Petition of Right (1628) (pp. 19–24); the English Bill of Rights (1689) (pp. 37–46); the American Bill of Rights (1789) and subsequent amendments to the Constitution (pp. 90–101).

From *Libertarianism: A Primer*: Chapter 9, "What Big Government Is All About" (pp. 186–209).

From *The Libertarian Reader*: Roger Pilon, "The Right to Do Wrong" (pp. 197–201).

Suggested Additional Reading

The Rights Retained by the People: The History and Meaning of the Ninth Amendment, Randy E. Barnett, ed. (Fairfax, Va.: George Mason University Press, 1989). The Ninth Amendment to the Constitution reads: "The enumeration in the Constitution of certain Rights shall not be construed to deny or disparage others retained by the people." This collection of historical documents and articles by legal scholars shows how the Ninth Amendment places checks on the power of government.

Leonard Levy, *The Emergence of a Free Press* (Oxford: Oxford University Press, 1985). Despite focusing principally on the First Amendment to the Constitution, this book offers valuable historical background to the Bill of Rights generally. Especially useful are Chapters 6 ("On the Eve of the American Revolution") and 7 ("From the Revolution to the First Amendment").

Herbert J. Storing, *What the Anti-Federalists Were For: The Political Thought of the Opponents of the Constitution* (Chicago: University of Chicago Press, 1981). Storing offers a synoptic view of the Anti-Federalist arguments and concerns and makes it clear that the Anti-Federalists were important shapers of the American constitutional system; the chapter of special relevance to the present module is Chapter 8, "Bill of Rights" (pp. 64–70).

For Further Study

James Bovard, *Lost Rights: The Destruction of American Liberty* (New York: St. Martin's, 1994). Bovard documents the active disregard for the Bill of Rights under current policies. This book reveals the great distance between the law of the land—the U.S. Constitution, as amended—and the "laws" issued by Congress, federal executive-branch agencies, and state and local governments.

Michael P. Zuckert, *Natural Rights and the New Republicanism* (Princeton: Princeton University Press, 1994). This book shows the roots of Whig and natural law thinking about the ends and limits of political power and how those were extended and developed by the American Founders.

The Bill of Rights: A Documentary History, Bernard Schwartz, ed. (New York: Chelsea House, 1971). This two-volume set includes the various precursor documents to the Bill of Rights, as well as excerpts from the correspondence of Madison, Jefferson, and others. Schwartz has also written a history of the Bill of Rights, *The Great Rights of Mankind: A History of the American Bill of Rights*, 2d ed. (Madison, Wisc.: Madison House, 1992).

Some Problems to Ponder

- Why list rights if no exhaustive list could be written? And why list activities and powers forbidden to government if those powers are not authorized in the first place? Is the Bill of Rights a redundancy in the Constitution?
- How are "natural rights" related to "legal rights" and "procedural rights"?
- Is it "undemocratic" to limit by law what the people may do?
- How can law limit itself?
- What good are "parchment barriers" to tyranny?
- What other items might you have added to the Bill of Rights, especially considering the experience of the years following the ratification of the Bill of Rights?
- Would an amendment to the Constitution limiting the terms of office of members of Congress (the president is already limited to two terms) help to secure limited government?
- The Ninth Amendment ("The enumeration in the Constitution of certain Rights shall not be construed to deny or disparage others retained by the people") speaks of other rights retained by the people. What might those other rights be?
- In Article I, Section 8, of the Constitution, the Congress is empowered to "provide for the common Defence and general Welfare of the United States." How is this related to the Tenth Amendment ("The powers not delegated to the United States by the Constitution, nor prohibited by it to the States, are reserved to the states respectively or to the people")?

Module 8: John Stuart Mill's *On Liberty* and Mary Wollstonecraft's *Vindication of the Rights of Woman*

Mary Wollstonecraft (1759–1797) is increasingly acknowledged as one of the most influential thinkers on women's rights and also as an incisive and observant writer on politics, education, and social issues. Although not consistently libertarian, she was consistently in favor of equal legal rights for men and women, and she operated within a generally classical liberal framework. The audiocassette presents an account of her life as a radical individualist writer as well as discussion of her arguments for equality before the law. In her writings she engaged some of the central issues in political philosophy, notably the debate over whether it was preferable to defend historically situated ("prescriptive") rights or universal ("abstract") rights. Burke had defended prescriptive rights but was highly critical of abstract statements of rights and therefore was wary about the application of rights theory to other candidates for rights (for example, women).

Among Wollstonecraft's more interesting observations is that the characters of subservient wives and of subservient soldiers are similar: both are taught to please and both live only to please. As belief in a "divine right of kings" perverts the character of kings, so, Wollstonecraft argued, belief in the "divine right of husbands" perverts the character of husbands.

The readings by Wollstonecraft and by the sisters Sarah and Angelina Grimké in this module focus on the relationship between rights and responsibilities. One cannot reasonably expect a person to act responsibly if one does not accord to that person both the right and the responsibility of self-governance.

John Stuart Mill (1806–1873), one of the best known intellectual figures of the nineteenth century, is especially revered by civil libertarians (as well as by Margaret Thatcher) for his essay *On Liberty*, published in 1859. Mill's principal concern was to ensure that individual liberty was not swallowed up in the move toward popular sovereignty. The emergence of the United States as a democratic republic led him to conclude, "It was now perceived that such phrases as 'self-government,' and 'the power of the people over themselves,' do not express the true state of the case. The 'people' who exercise the power are not always the same people with those over whom it is exercised; and the 'self-government' spoken of is not the government of each by himself, but of each by all the rest." Mill's account of the need to protect individual liberty from "the tyranny of the majority" has been highy influential—notably his defense of freedom of speech as a process of determining the truth; being "protected" from falsehood is the same as being "protected" from the possibility of knowing truth.

The readings from Mill and from Boaz explore the meaning of individual liberty and responsibility for one's own moral development, and the chapters by the distinguished jurist Bruno Leoni consider different meanings of freedom and constraint. Leoni parts company with Mill on the question of whether freedom should be construed principally as freedom from coercion by the state or as freedom from "social pressure" as well. Mill had argued in *On Liberty* that "protection . . . against the tyranny of the magistrate is not enough; there needs protection also against the tyranny of the prevailing opinion and feeling, against the tendency of society to impose, by other means than civil penalties, its own ideas and practices as rules of conduct on those who dissent from them." Others, such as Bruno Leoni, have argued that liberty should not be confused with freedom from public opinion but should be limited to freedom from coercion, understood in terms of force or the threat of force.

Milton Friedman, in the excerpt from *Capitalism and Freedom*, argues that private property and a capitalist economy are necessary prerequisites for individuality, freedom of speech, and Mill's "experiments in living." David Boaz, in the chapters from his book, considers the dignity and worth of the individual human being and the possibility of the coexistence of individuals of different faiths, philosophies, and cultures in a free and open society.

This module treats the issues of equal rights, especially with reference to women and to the flourishing of individuality and pluralism in a free society. The grounding of the libertarian view in individual rights, rather than in collective claims, provides important insights into the contemporary debate on "multiculturalism."

Readings to Accompany These Tapes

From *The Libertarian Reader*: Alexis de Tocqueville, "What Sort of Despotism Democratic Nations Have to Fear" (pp. 20–24); John Stuart Mill, "Objections to Government Interference" (pp. 25–27), "Of Individuality" (pp. 96–103); Mary Wollstonecraft, "The Subjugation of Women" (pp. 62–64); Angelina Grimké, "Rights and Responsibilities of Women" (pp. 92–93); Sarah Grimké, "Woman as a Moral Being" (pp. 94–95); Milton Friedman, "The Relation between Economic Freedom and Political Freedom" (pp. 292–302).

From *Libertarianism: A Primer*: Chapter 4, "The Dignity of the Individual" (pp. 94–104); Chapter 5, "Pluralism and Toleration" (pp. 105–14).

From *Freedom and the Law*: Introduction (pp. 3–25); Chapter 1, "Which Freedom" (pp. 26–42); Chapter 2, "'Freedom' and 'Constraint'" (pp. 43–57).

Suggested Additional Reading

Albert Jay Nock, "On Doing the Right Thing," in Albert Jay Nock, *The State of the Union: Essays in Social Criticism*, Charles H. Hamilton, ed. (Indianapolis: Liberty Press, 1991), and in *Our Enemy the State*, Walter E. Grinder, ed. (1935; San Francisco: Fox & Wilkes, 1994). This essay makes the case for individual liberty and responsibility very eloquently; both of the editions listed include other valuable works by Nock, as well as useful introductions to Nock's thought by the editors.

John Stuart Mill, *On Liberty* (many editions). One can still profit from a close reading of this classic work. One especially noteworthy feature is the way in which Mill considers both state coercion and what he calls "the despotism of culture" enemies of liberty. As Thomas Babington Macaulay noted, this feature of Mill's argument seems the weakest, although it is often advanced by modern liberals as the strongest part of Mill's argument.

Mary Wollstonecraft, *A Vindication of the Rights of Men* and *A Vindication of the Rights of Woman* (many editions). Wollstonecraft argued vehemently for equality of legal rights and liabilities, even if she was not always arguing for a strictly libertarian set of rights. (Her

41

views on state education and the virtues of the Spartans were certainly incompatible with a considered classical liberal view, but her emphasis was on the equal treatment of men and women by the state.)

Herbert Spencer, *Social Statics* (1850; New York: Robert Schalkenbach Foundation, 1995). This is a brilliant and highly influential statement of the ethical foundations of a free and progressive society. It includes Spencer's criticism of utilitarianism, which he termed the "expediency philosophy."

For Further Study

Freedom, Feminism, and the State, Wendy McElroy, ed. (Washington: Cato Institute, 1982). This collection brings together many of the most influential writings of the individualist feminist movement and includes a valuable introductory essay by the editor.

Wilhelm von Humboldt, *The Limits of State Action* (1792; Indianapolis: Liberty Press, 1993). This book exercised a powerful influence on John Stuart Mill, as well as on the general direction of the moral sciences in the nineteenth century. Humboldt was a brilliant Prussian liberal who set his ideas out to, as he put it in the opening words of the book, "discover to what end State institutions should be directed, and what limits should be set to their activity." Humboldt's treatment of liberty is less ambiguous than Mill's better known work.

Lysander Spooner, *Vices Are Not Crimes* (1875), reprinted in *The Lysander Spooner Reader*, George H. Smith, ed. (San Francisco: Fox & Wilkes, 1992). This essay originally appeared in a volume titled *Prohibition: A Failure*, long before the horrible experiences of what we now know as the Prohibition Era. This essay shines the light of reason on the attempts of government to use coercion to punish vice.

Some Problems to Ponder

- What is the relationship between responsibility for one's behavior and the right and freedom to direct that behavior?
- Do equal legal rights for men and women entail equality in all other respects?

- If an act such as excessive alcohol drinking is harmful to the person who undertakes it, or to others in his or her life (such as a spouse or children), in what sense is the act "victimless"?
- Is it contrary to individualist principles for some people (whether a majority or a minority) to criticize the behavior or choices of others, if they refrain from resorting to force or legal coercion?
- Is there a difference between an immoral act and a criminal act? Are all criminal acts immoral? Are all immoral acts criminal?
- How can people become virtuous if the state does not direct them toward virtue?
- Can freedom of speech and the press exist without private property?

Module 9: Henry David Thoreau's *Civil Disobedience* and William Lloyd Garrison's *The Liberator*

Henry David Thoreau (1817–1862), perhaps best known as the author of *Walden*, was a deep believer in the demands of conscience over the demands of the state. His refusal in July 1846 to pay a tax led him to write the essay *Civil Disobedience*, which was to exercise a great influence on subsequent generations of thinkers. This module explores political obligation generally, including the questions of whether one should submit to unjust demands from political authorities and whether a citizen should acquiesce when the state makes him or her "the agent of injustice to another." Thoreau draws on a long libertarian tradition that holds that, although our universal, or general, obligations are not the result of choice or action (for example, the obligation not to take the life, liberty, or justly held possessions of any other person), particular obligations, that is, specific obligations to specific persons, are based on some act of the obligee, for example, assenting to a contract that requires the payment of a sum of money for a service rendered. Obligations to pay taxes to the state or to submit to its authority normally fall into the second category of particular obligations. Thoreau insists that he did not consent to them, and that he therefore is not bound by them and instead follows the demands of his own conscience (notably his opposition to the enforcement of slavery and to the war with Mexico).

In effect, Thoreau insists on a right to withdraw from the state, a right also articulated by Herbert Spencer in his essay "The Right to Ignore the State" in the readings for this module. Thoreau sought to live as a wholly free person in a world that was not wholly free. David Boaz, in his chapter "The Obsolete State," speculates that the growth of the market and the spread of new technologies may allow individuals greater opportunity in the future to "bypass the state."

Of overriding importance to Thoreau was his refusal to sanction the evil institution of slavery, and thus his violation of the Fugitive Slave Laws and his participation in the Underground Railway to freedom for escaped slaves. While Thoreau opposed slavery, his principal response was to resist it passively, rather than to crusade for its abolition. In contrast, William Lloyd Garrison (1805–1879) was moved to devote all of his energy and resources to a tireless crusade for abolition. In response to those who criticized him for his enthusiasm, he retorted, "I have need to be all on fire, for there are mountains of ice around me to melt." His "immediatism" was realistic but uncompromising: "We have never said that slavery would be overthrown by a single blow; that it ought to be, we shall always contend." (It bears mentioning, however, that while Garrison criticized John Brown for his attempt to liberate the slaves through a slave uprising, Thoreau defended Brown, writing, "No man in America has ever stood up so persistently and effectively for the dignity of human nature, knowing himself for a man, and the equal of any and all governments. In that sense, he was the most American of us all.")

The readings by Garrison, Frederick Douglass, and William Ellery Channing argue that slavery violates the fundamental equal right of all individuals to be free. The readings from Immanuel Kant and from Bruno Leoni argue that the internal logic of law requires that law be equally applicable to all, a requirement that chattel slavery notoriously fails, and one that many lesser infringements on liberty may fail as well.

Readings to Accompany These Tapes

From *The Libertarian Reader*: William Lloyd Garrison, "Man Cannot Hold Property in Man" (pp. 77–80); Frederick Douglass, "You Are a Man, and So Am I" (pp. 81–87); William Ellery Channing, "A Human Being Cannot Be Justly Owned" (pp. 88–91); Herbert Spencer, "The Right to Ignore the State" (pp. 149–53); Immanuel Kant, "Equality of Rights" (pp. 142–48); Lysander Spooner, "The Constitution of No Authority" (pp. 154–60).

From *Libertarianism: A Primer*: Chapter 11, "The Obsolete State" (pp. 256–75).

From *Freedom and the Law*: Chapter 3, "Freedom and the Rule of Law" (pp. 58–75).

Suggested Additional Reading

Henry David Thoreau, *Political Writings,* Nancy L. Rosenblum, ed. (Cambridge: Cambridge University Press, 1996) contains, in addition to his essay on civil disobedience (titled "Resistance to Civil Government" in this edition), "Life without Principle," "Slavery in Massachusetts," his essays on John Brown, and selections from *Walden.* Thoreau reminds us that the state can punish the body but the human spirit remains capable of freedom. As he said of his incarceration for his refusal to pay a tax: "I did not for a moment feel confined, and the walls seemed a great waste of stone and mortar. . . . I could not but smile to see how industriously they locked the door on my meditations, which followed them out again without let or hindrance. As they could not reach me, they resolved to punish my body; just as boys, if they cannot come against a person against whom they have a spite, will abuse his dog. I saw that the state was half-witted, that it was as timid as a lone woman with her silver spoons. . . . I lost all my remaining respect for it, and pitied it."

Aileen S. Kraditor, *Means and Ends in American Abolitionism: Garrison and His Critics on Strategy and Tactics, 1834–1850* (Chicago: Ivan R. Dee, 1989). This book examines the debates over how to eliminate slavery, with a central focus on the radical approach of William Lloyd Garrison. Kraditor discusses how such issues as moral suasion, civil disobedience, electoral activism, and slave rebellions were debated and action was taken.

For Further Study

Jennifer Trusted, *Free Will and Responsibility* (Oxford: Oxford University Press, 1984). For those interested in the deep connection drawn by rights theorists between personal choice and responsibility, which motivated the early rights theorists, the Abolitionists, and the individualist feminists of the nineteenth century, this book offers a careful examination of the philosophical issues involved. Libertarianism, understood as the theory that individuals can initiate actions and responsibility for action can be traced back to the individual, is neatly contrasted with determinism, understood as the view that our behavior is entirely determined by external factors, with a corresponding lack of personal moral responsibility for behavior. The book is written in an accessible style and does not require any extensive philosphical background.

Frank Chodorov, *Fugitive Essays*, Charles H. Hamilton, ed. (Indianapolis: Liberty Press, 1980). In addition to containing a moving essay on Henry David Thoreau, this book is full of wisdom about how a free man might live in a world only partially free. Chodorov wrote a very provocative and insightful little essay, "Don't Buy Bonds" (reprinted in his *Out of Step: The Autobiography of an Individualist* [New York: Devin-Adair, 1962], which is unfortunately no longer in print).

Lewis Perry, *Radical Abolitionism: Anarchy and the Government of God in Antislavery Thought* (Knoxville: University of Tennessee Press, 1995). Perry focuses on the more radical abolitionists, many of whom rejected slavery on the same grounds that they rejected absolute government.

Some Problems to Ponder

- Some proponents of abolishing slavery favored compensating the slaveholders for loss of their slaves. Others argued that it was the slaves who deserved compensation for the loss of their liberty. Which position is more just? Which is more practical?
- Would secession by the Northern states from the Union have been justified as a means of eliminating the Fugitive Slave Laws?
- What should a conscientious citizen do when the demands of the state conflict with the moral voice of conscience?
- Can one actually "mind one's own business" in a complex society? Can individuals withdraw from politics?
- How can a formal requirement of equality before the law or of certainty in the law generate substantive constraints on law?
- Henry David Thoreau survived his passive resistance to the American state, as Gandhi did his to British colonial rule, but would they have been so lucky under a National Socialist or Communist state? Does the character of the state determine the appropriate response to it?

Module 10: The Achievements of Nineteenth-Century Classical Liberalism

During the nineteenth century the principles of individual liberty, constitutionally limited government, peace, and reliance on the institutions of civil society and the free market for social order and economic prosperity were fused together into a powerful synthesis, known as liberalism. Although the term "liberalism" retains its original meaning in most of the world, it has unfortunately come to have a very different meaning in late twentieth-century America. Hence terms such as "market liberalism," "classical liberalism," or "libertarianism" are often used in its place in America. This module shows how liberalism developed in Europe and America in the nineteenth century. In addition to examining the important debates, such as those between utilitarians and natural rights advocates and between supporters and opponents of state involvement in education, this module traces the rise and the ultimate collapse of liberalism. By the end of the nineteenth century, liberalism had all but died as an intellectual and political movement. It was replaced by various forms of collectivism, such as socialism, fascism, racism, nationalism, imperialism, and corporatism. (The revival and reformulation of liberalism after World War II are covered in the next two modules.)

A number of fascinating chapters in the story of liberalism are developed at length in this module, including the opposition to mercantilism, coercive monopolies, and special privileges; the rise and success of the Anti–Corn Law League and of the general movement for free trade; the vigorous debates over state education; and the liberal theory of progress. A lengthy examination of the ideas of one of the great figures of nineteenth-century liberalism, Herbert Spencer, gives insight into both the rise and the fall of liberalism, for Spencer was active during both periods. The ideas of a formidable American liberal, the sociologist William Graham Sumner, who warned of the consequences of abandoning the ideal of limited government and respect for the equal rights of individuals, also receive careful consideration. Each chapter bears important lessons for modern-day libertarians.

Of special significance are the remarkable efforts of the French liberal Frederic Bastiat, who explained in remarkably clear language the fallacies of socialist and interventionist thinking. Bastiat, whom Joseph Schumpeter called "the greatest economic journalist who ever lived," used devastating wit and logic to reveal the errors of protectionist, Keynesian (before Keynes was even born), interventionist, and socialist arguments. He insisted that the good economist is concerned to show, not only the direct effects of a policy, but the indirect ones, as well. Adam Smith had devoted great attention to showing the indirect, or unintended, effects of market exchanges; as he argued in *The Wealth of Nations*, we do not intend to create a complex social order when we exchange, but that is the result of our action. Bastiat concentrated on showing the indirect effects of state intervention. The American economist Henry Hazlitt, formerly a columnist for the *New York Times* and for *Newsweek*, updated that lesson and applied it to American institutions in *Economics in One Lesson*.

Alexis de Tocqueville, in the reading from his famous *Democracy in America*, shows how freedom and virtue were made compatible in the America of his day. Richard Cobden, whose work on behalf of freedom of trade and international peace is examined in the audiotapes, explains in the selections from his writings how peace promotes international harmony. And the essay from a 1900 issue of *The Nation* foretells the future with chilling accuracy: "We hear no more of natural rights, but of inferior races, whose part it is to submit to the government of those whom God has made their superiors. The old fallacy of divine right has once more asserted its ruinous power, and before it is again repudiated there must be international struggles on a terrific scale."

Readings to Accompany These Tapes

From *The Libertarian Reader*: Richard Cobden, "Commerce Is the Great Panacea" (pp. 319–20), "Nonintervention" (pp. 322–23); *The Nation*, "The Eclipse of Liberalism" (pp. 324–26); Alexis de Tocqueville, "Interest Rightly Understood" (pp. 75–76); Frederic Bastiat, "What Is Seen and What Is Not Seen" (pp. 265–73).

From *Economics in One Lesson*: Chapter 1, "The Lesson" (pp. 3–10);
Chapter 2, "The Broken Window" (pp. 11–12); Chapter 3, "The
Blessings of Destruction" (pp. 13–18); Chapter 4, "Public Works
Mean Taxes" (pp. 19–24); Chapter 5, "Taxes Discourage Production" (pp. 25–26); Chapter 6, "Credit Diverts Production"
(pp. 27–34); Chapter 11, "Who's 'Protected' by Tariffs?"
(pp. 59–69); Chapter 12, "The Drive for Exports" (pp. 70–74).

From *How the West Grew Rich*: Chapter 5, "The Development of
Industry" (pp. 144–88); Chapter 6, "Diversity of Organization:
The Corporation" (pp. 189–210).

Suggested Additional Reading

Ralph Raico, *Classical Liberalism: Historical Essays in Political Economy*
(New York: Routledge, 1998). This selection of essays is probably
the most valuable recent work on the legacy of classical liberalism.
In addition to presenting pioneering work, the author is a master
of English prose.

Frederic Bastiat, *Selected Essays on Political Economy*, ed. George B.
De Huszar (Irvington-on-Hudson, N.Y.: Foundation for Economic
Education, 1964). Frederic Bastiat was perhaps the clearest writer
on political economy ever to set pen to paper. His brilliant essay
"What Is Seen and What Is Not Seen" is essential reading for
an understanding of economics (it is excerpted in *The Libertarian
Reader*), and his essays "The Law" and "The State" (in which he
noted that "the state is the great fictitious entity by which everyone
seeks to live at the expense of everyone else") are works of genius.

Herbert Spencer, *The Man vs. the State*. We are fortunate that there
are currently two editions of this work in print: *The Man vs. the
State, with Six Essays on Government, Society, and Freedom*, foreword
by Eric Mack and introduction by Albert Jay Nock (Indianapolis:
Liberty Press, 1982); and *Political Writings of Herbert Spencer*, John
Offer, ed. (Cambridge: Cambridge University Press, 1994). These
essays offer Spencer's mature reflections on the decline of liberalism toward the end of the nineteenth century and his proposals
for reinvigorating it. Notably, he concluded his essay "The Great
Political Superstition" with the observation: "The function of Liberalism in the past was that of putting a limit to the powers of
kings. The function of true Liberalism in the future will be that
of putting a limit to the powers of Parliaments."

Western Liberalism: A History in Documents from Locke to Croce, E. K.
Bramsted and K. J. Melhuish, eds. (New York: Longman, 1978).
This brilliant collection includes both classical liberal writings and
some "revisionist" or "modern" liberal writings, such as those of
T. H. Green and John Maynard Keynes.

For Further Study

*On Liberty, Society, and Politics: The Essential Essays of William Graham
Sumner*, Robert C. Bannister, ed. (Indianapolis: Liberty Press,
1992). This outstanding collection of Sumner's writings includes
his prescient essay on the corroding effects of foreign adventurism
on republican institutions, "The Conquest of the United States by
Spain" (1898); his defense of the taxpayer, "The Forgotten Man"
(1883); and his defense of the presumption of liberty, "Laissez
Faire" (1886).

*Herbert Spencer and the Limits of the State: The Late Nineteenth-Century
Debate between Individualism and Collectivism*, Michael Taylor, ed.
(Bristol, U.K.: Thoemmes Press, 1996). This collection of original
essays brilliantly documents the issues at stake in the debate
between individualists and collectivists in the nineteenth century.
In his introduction, the editor shows how current debates over
the welfare state, socialism, and constitutional limits on state
power are largely continuations of debates of the previous century.

Capitalism and the Historians, F. A. Hayek, ed. (Chicago: University
of Chicago Press, 1954). This collection of essays examines the
remarkable hostility toward capitalism and industrialism among
intellectuals and compares their pronouncements with the available historical record. Although much valuable historical research
has been done in the years since this collection was published,
this little volume retains its value.

Some Problems to Ponder

- If it is necessary to bring people to understand both "what is
  seen" and "what is not seen" if they are to embrace the free
  society, are libertarians at a disadvantage compared to statists,
  who can always point out that someone reaps positive benefits
  that can be attributed to the statist interventions? If there is a
  natural disadvantage because of the necessarily abstract nature
  of libertarian political economy, how might that be overcome?

- Was the extension of the franchise a cause of the decline of liberalism or a mechanism to secure the gains that liberals had made against the "sinister interests" of those with power?
- Would the efforts of the Anti–Corn Law League have been successful in eliminating tariffs if there had not been a famine in Ireland? What is the relationship between the activities and intentions of political reformers, such as the liberal crusaders for freedom of trade, and external factors? How does one know when there are opportunities to advance liberal principles and which fights one should fight?
- How do the insights of Bastiat concerning the "seen and the unseen" refute the fallacies behind such doctrines as "the balance of trade," "anti-dumping laws," and "wartime prosperity"?
- If a population educated in the principles of liberalism—respect for individual rights, understanding of the constitutional limitations on state power, and so on—is necessary for those principles to be sustained, is state education to impart those principles appropriate? If not, how would one diffuse the principles of liberalism sufficiently widely throughout the population to sustain the free society?
- A newspaper article on the boom in the construction industry in south Florida after a hurricane is headlined, "Hurricane Andrew Good News for South Florida Economy." The boost for the construction industry is "seen." What is not seen?
- In the 1960s it was popular to assert that Germany and Japan had become rich in the postwar era because all of their factories had been destroyed in the war, allowing them to rebuild new and more technologically advanced factories. The conclusion seemed to be that bombing American factories would make America richer. What is wrong with that argument?
- How do modern libertarians avoid the fate of late-nineteenth-century liberals, who failed to stop the onslaught of collectivism and war?

Module 11: The "Austrian" Case for the Free Market

This module explores the contributions made to the understanding of liberty by the "Austrian" economists, mainly Ludwig von Mises (1871–1973) and F. A. Hayek (1899–1992). In the 1920s and for many years thereafter, Mises was one of a handful of scholars willing to criticize collectivism in general and socialist economic planning in particular. He was reviled and scorned for his work, but recent years have seen almost universal, albeit grudging, acknowledgment that he was right: socialism cannot solve the problem of economic calculation. As Mises noted, "Socialism is the abolition of rational economy." A market economy based on private property is necessary to generate the prices on the basis of which resources can be allocated among competing uses. Mises's book *Socialism*, published in 1922, marked a turning point in the intellectual battle against full-scale collectivism. As F. A. Hayek later noted, "When *Socialism* first appeared in 1922, its impact was profound. It gradually but fundamentally altered the outlook of many of the young idealists returning to their university studies after World War I. I know, for I was one of them. . . . Socialism promised to fulfill our hopes for a more rational, more just world. And then came this book. Our hopes were dashed." The victims of socialism suffered for years before Mises's arguments were accepted generally.

The critique of socialism launched an enormous investigation of how markets actually work. Model builders who merely included prices in their models and then assumed that prices adjust automatically overlooked the crucial problem of the decentralization of knowledge (described in Hayek's essay "The Use of Knowledge in Society," which is included in the readings for this module) and the central role of the profit-seeking entrepreneur in adjusting prices. Mises and Hayek insisted that to assume away the problem of explaining how prices are adjusted was to assume away the economic problem itself. There can be no useful prices without private property, freedom of contract, and the right to the profits accruing to entrepreneurial activity. (These issues are examined by Henry Hazlitt in the excerpts from *Economics in One Lesson* for this module.)

Both Mises and Hayek drew on their study of economic processes to build a wider case for the liberty of the individual under limited, constitutional government. Hayek devoted great attention to understanding the proper role of law in guaranteeing rights and became convinced that law itself was a discovery process, analogous to the market process. Just as market institutions evolve, so the legal order is the result of an evolutionary process. The market is a spontaneous order that cannot be planned in advance. The institutions of the market, from legal rules to contractual forms to firms, are also the result of evolutionary processes, as the legal scholar Bruno Leoni explains in the chapters from his book *Freedom and the Law*. The evolution of forms of business enterprise is considered in the chapter from *How the West Grew Rich*, by Rosenberg and Birdzell.

Note: In the audiocassettes it is mentioned that Mises did not live to witness the growth of interest in his ideas. It should also be mentioned that he did not live to see the destruction of the Soviet Union, which also took place after these audiocassettes were recorded. (Hence the mention of Mises's birthplace of Lemberg, "now ironically the city of Lvov in the Soviet Union.")

Readings to Accompany These Tapes

From *The Libertarian Reader*: Ludwig von Mises, "On Equality and Inequality" (pp. 104–7), "Socialism and Interventionism" (pp. 274–85), "Peace" (pp. 327–30); F. A. Hayek, "The Use of Knowledge in Society" (pp. 215–24), "Made Orders and Spontaneous Orders" (pp. 233–42), "The Market Order or Catallaxy" (pp. 303–11); Michael Polanyi, "Two Kinds of Order" (pp. 225–32).

From *Freedom and the Law*: Chapter 4, "Freedom and the Certainty of the Law" (pp. 76–94); Chapter 5, "Freedom and Legislation" (pp. 95–111); Postscript, "The Law as Individual Claim" (pp. 189–203).

From *Economics in One Lesson*: Chapter 15, "How the Price System Works" (pp. 87–93); Chapter 22, "The Function of Profits" (pp. 144–48).

From *How the West Grew Rich*: Chapter 9, "Diversity of Enterprise" (pp. 269–301).

Suggested Additional Reading

Ludwig von Mises, *Human Action* (New Haven: Yale University Press, 1963, and later editions). This is an immensely rewarding book; it is also a rather difficult and challenging one. Rather than merely a treatise on economics, it is a general treatment of the problems of social coordination.

Murray N. Rothbard, *Man, Economy, and State* (Los Angeles: Nash Publishing, 1970). Like *Human Action*, this book is a sweeping treatise on the science of economics, but it is generally more accessible to American readers. It starts with fundamental principles, such as the principle of choice and the concept of the marginal unit of choice, and develops a coherent science of human cooperation and coordination.

F. A. Hayek, *The Essential Hayek*, Chiaki Nishiyama and Kurt R. Leube, eds. (Stanford: Hoover Institution Press, 1984). Hayek wrote many books and essays and numerous editions are available. This one brings together in one volume contributions to economics, the theory of knowledge, political philosophy, and intellectual history.

For Further Study

F. A. Hayek, *The Fatal Conceit* (Chicago: University of Chicago Press, 1988). This, Hayek's last book, is a synthesis of his life's work.

Ludwig von Mises, *Socialism* (1922; Indianapolis: Liberty Press, 1981). This is Mises's classic critique of socialism, notable not only for his argument about the impossibility of socialist economic calculation but also for his sociological and philosophical insights into socialism.

Ludwig von Mises, *Bureaucracy* (1944; Irvington-on-Hudson, N.Y.: Foundation for Economic Education, 1984). As a complement to his analysis of socialism, Mises examined the differences between the organizing principles of voluntary institutions operating within the market and government bureaucracies.

Israel Kirzner, *Discovery and the Capitalist Process* (Chicago: University of Chicago Press, 1985). Kirzner refines the notion of entrepreneurship, explains the role of the entrepreneur as the moving force of a market economy, and applies those insights to taxation and regulatory policies.

Chandran Kukathas, *Hayek and Modern Liberalism* (Oxford: Oxford University Press, 1989). Kukathas offers an excellent general overview of Hayek's political philosophy.

Some Problems to Ponder

- If markets and prices serve to coordinate the activities of the participants in a complex economy, why are there firms?
- What does it mean to say that in an advanced economy production is "roundabout"? Why are free prices and interest rates necessary to regulate a complex and roundabout system of production?
- How do prices adjust in a market economy? What role is played by the profit-seeking entrepreneur?
- In what ways can interventionism be self-defeating? How does one intervention lead to another?
- What is the difference between cost and price, and which determines which?
- What kind of knowledge do prices convey?
- If, as Hayek argues, our morals are not the product of our reason, what role can reason play in criticizing moral claims, for example, the moral claims made on behalf of socialism?

Module 12: The Modern Quest for Liberty

The final module of the Cato University curriculum examines the rebirth of libertarian thought from the 1940s onward. The collapse of classical liberalism in the face of both the collectivist intellectual assault on civilization and its own internal flaws and conflicts (especially notable is the debate between utilitarians and natural-rights advocates) is presented as background to the story of the remarkable people who brought libertarian thinking back from the dead. Their insights and activities are both inspiring and instructive. They had the courage and the foresight to undertake a long-term defense of civilization against the collectivist assault.

In an age when the moral superiority of collectivism was almost universally taken for granted, and pleas for socialistic reform were tempered only by the concession that humans may not yet be good enough for socialism, these libertarian pioneers affirmed the moral goodness of the free society. They drew on a long tradition of libertarian thought to refine and greatly advance the case for liberty. (The audiotape points out that "in recent years many scholarly treatments of the libertarian tradition have been published." Many of these are listed in earlier Cato University modules; a good volume that reveals the role of the tradition in forming American thought is Michael P. Zuckert, *Natural Rights and the New Republicanism*, mentioned in module 7, on the U.S. Constitution.)

The publication in 1943 of books by three American writers, Rose Wilder Lane (*The Discovery of Freedom*), Isabel Paterson (*The God of the Machine*), and Ayn Rand (*The Fountainhead*), all extolling the creativity of the free and responsible individual, and in 1944 of books by the Austrian economists Ludwig von Mises (*Omnipotent Government*) and F. A. Hayek (*The Road to Serfdom*), both warning of the dangers of statism, helped to launch the modern libertarian movement. It was crucially important that these writers all identified the various anti-libertarian movements of the time—fascism,

National Socialism (more popularly known as Nazism), socialism, communism, and the like—as growths from the same philosophical root: collectivism. The conflict between Hitler and Stalin, for example, rather than being a titanic struggle between different philosophies or world-views, was in reality a fight between two varieties of the same fundamental principle: that the individual exists entirely for the sake of the collective, whether the collective be a race, nation, or class.

The formation of the Mont Pèlerin Society in Switzerland in 1947 was to prove enormously influential in reviving libertarian ideas at the higher intellectual and academic levels, as a part of a conscious plan to diffuse libertarian principles throughout the general population. The spread of libertarian ideas and organizations around the world has accelerated since that time, promoted by visionary thinkers of the caliber of Milton Friedman and F. A. Hayek and by such institutions as the London-based Institute of Economic Affairs, founded in 1957, and the Washington-based Cato Institute, founded in 1977, which have devoted themselves to practical applications of libertarian principles.

David Boaz concludes his book *Libertarianism: A Primer,*

> As we enter a new century and a new millenium, we encounter a world of endless possibility. The very premise of the world of global markets and new technologies is libertarianism. Neither stultifying socialism nor rigid conservatism could produce the free, technologically advanced society that we anticipate in the twenty-first century. If we want a dynamic world of prosperity and opportunity, we must make it a libertarian world. The simple and timeless principles of the American Revolution—individual liberty, limited government, and free markets—turn out to be even more powerful in today's world of instant communication, global markets, and unprecedented access to information than Jefferson or Madison could have imagined. Libertarianism is not just a framework for utopia, it is the essential framework for the future.

Readings to Accompany These Tapes

From *The Libertarian Reader*: Isabel Paterson, "The Humanitarian with the Guillotine" (pp. 31–35); Douglas J. Den Uyl and Douglas B. Rasmussen, "Ayn Rand on Rights and Capitalism" (pp. 169–80); Alvin Toffler, "The Playboy Interview with Ayn Rand" (pp. 161–68); Murray N. Rothbard, "The State" (pp. 36–41); Michael Prowse, "Paternalist Government Is Out of Date" (pp. 388–92).

From *Libertarianism: A Primer*: Chapter 10, "Contemporary Issues" (pp. 210–55); Chapter 12, "The Libertarian Future" (pp. 276–89).

Suggested Additional Reading

John L. Kelley, *Bringing the Market Back In: The Political Revitalization of Market Liberalism* (New York: New York University Press, 1997). Written in an academic style, this rigorously researched book documents the revival of the classical liberal movement in America from the 1970s onward.

Ronald Max Hartwell, *A History of the Mont Pèlerin Society* (Indianapolis: Liberty Fund, 1995). Hartwell is a distinguished economic historian and past president of the Mont Pèlerin Society. He has applied his skills as a historian to writing the history of the MPS, documenting internal debates as well as its enormous influence.

Edward H. Crane, "Defending Civil Society," *Cato's Letter* No. 8 (Washington: Cato Institute, 1994). The president of the Cato Institute sounds a call for revitalizing and extending the scope of civil society and restraining political society.

F. A. Hayek, "The Intellectuals and Socialism," in F. A. Hayek, *Studies in Philosophy, Economics, and Politics* (Chicago: University of Chicago Press, 1967). In this essay Hayek lays out a long-term strategy for the revival of libertarianism. The essay, which originally appeared in 1949, concludes, "Unless we can make the philosophic foundations of a free society once more a living intellectual issue, and its implementation a task which challenges the ingenuity and imagination of our liveliest minds, the prospects of freedom are indeed dark. But if we can regain that belief in the power of ideas which was the mark of liberalism at its best, the battle is not lost. The intellectual revival of liberalism is already under way in many parts of the world. Will it be in time?"

For Further Study

The Essence of Friedman, Kurt Leube, ed. (Stanford: Hoover Institution Press, 1987). This is a useful collection of Friedman's writings on monetary economics, political economy, and other fields.

Murray N. Rothbard, *For a New Liberty: The Libertarian Manifesto* (New York: Macmillan, 1978). This book is a coherent and popularized statement of Rothbard's political philosophy.

Ayn Rand, *Capitalism: The Unknown Ideal* (New York: Penguin, 1967), with additional articles by Nathaniel Branden, Alan Greenspan, and Robert Hessen. This is one of the best collections of the individualist writings of Ayn Rand, defending the morality of the free market, glorifying the entrepreneurial creator, and denouncing statism. It includes her two essays "Man's Rights" and "The Nature of Government."

Rose Wilder Lane, *The Discovery of Freedom: Man's Struggle against Authority* (1943; San Francisco: Fox & Wilkes, 1984). This withering attack on statism, nationalism, and authoritarianism helped to launch the modern libertarian movement. Lane was an excellent and inspiring writer whose book offers a sweeping view of the 6,000-year struggle of ordinary people to raise their families, produce food, develop industries, pursue commerce, and in myriad ways improve human life—all in defiance of their rulers. Lane especially celebrates the American Revolution, which showed dramatically how ordinary people could achieve extraordinary freedom and tells us how we can reclaim the promise of America.

Milton Friedman, *Capitalism and Freedom* (Chicago: University of Chicago Press, 1962). This book changed the thinking of countless people who, through its pages, came to understand the intimate relationship between the free market and personal liberty.

Some Problems to Ponder

- Rose Wilder Lane said that her rejection of communism and embrace of libertarianism came from her visits to Transcaucasian Russia after the Bolshevik coup d'état. F. A. Hayek said that his rejection of socialism and embrace of libertarianism came after reading Ludwig von Mises's book *Socialism*. Are people more likely to learn about liberty from abstract arguments, as presented in books, for example, or from concrete experience of the failures of statism?
- If rights are a good thing to have, why not have more of them? The welfare state promises ever more rights—to food, shelter, housing, and so forth. Isn't this an improvement?

- Why did classical liberalism fade out? Is it again on the upswing? How might modern libertarians avoid the fate of the classical liberals?
- How deep do philosophical agreements have to run for people to agree on libertarianism as a political philosophy? Can people of different faiths or of no faith share common principles of morality and justice?
- Are some cultures more conducive to liberty than others? What values are most likely to comport well with libertarianism?
- How do we get from "here" to a fully free, or at least a freer, society? What role do political reforms (for example, term limits or a balanced-budget amendment) play? What role do academic research and argument play? What role do "think tanks" play?

Conclusion

The twelve-module Cato University curriculum provides a general overview of the tradition of libertarianism and of the rich insights it provides into social, economic, cultural, and political life. The Cato Institute is dedicated, not only to preserving, but to extending, refining, and applying the insights of the libertarians of the past. We hope that you have enjoyed this curriculum of Cato University and that you will continue your involvement with the Cato Institute.

About the Author

Tom G. Palmer is director of special projects at the Cato Institute. He was very active in the late 1980s and the early 1990s in the propagation of classical liberal ideas and the revival of civil society in the Soviet bloc states and their successors. He holds a B.A. in liberal arts from St. John's College in Annapolis, Maryland, and an M.A. in philosophy from The Catholic University of America in Washington, D.C. He is currently an H. B. Earhart Fellow at Hertford College, Oxford University, where he is completing his D.Phil. in politics. Before joining the Cato Institute, Palmer was a vice president of the Institute for Humane Studies at George Mason University. He regularly lectures in America and Europe on the scientific study of politics, the relationship between individualism and civil society, the functions of property and the market, and the moral and legal foundations of individual rights. He has published articles on politics and morality in scholarly journals such as the *Harvard Journal of Law and Public Policy* and *Constitutional Political Economy*, as well as in newspapers such as the *Wall Street Journal*, the *New York Times*, and the *Washington Post*.